hope stories

courageously trusting in God's perfect timing

KW
KingdomWinds
PUBLISHING

First Edition, 2023
ISBN: 978-1-64590-040-5
Published by Kingdom Winds Publishing.
www.kingdomwinds.com
publishing@kingdomwinds.com
Printed in the United States of America.

Table of Contents

From the Founder 5
[Nicole Clark]

Sarah 7
[Stephanie Hanrahan]

Rebekah 15
[Lisbeth Van Daalen]

Rachel 23
[Sarah Blakeney]

Elizabeth 33
[Anitha Thomas Abrams]

Hannah 41
[Becky Bierwas]

Shunammite Woman, part 1 53
[Lindsey Jensen]

Shunammite Woman, part 2 61
[Lindsey Jensen]

from the founder

Nicole Clark

Hope, it's woven into each lesson of this study. I pray the lessons shine the steadfast light of the One who never leaves our side. Traveling throughout His word, we've intertwined stories of pain and resilience, fear and faith, desperation and hope.

Twelve 12 Ministries exists to bring women together, strengthening relationships with Christ. The heart behind Hope is to remind you that you are seen, loved, and not forgotten. We walk through pain together with God guiding our paths.

My personal story is one of infertility, heartbreak, and miscarriage. In the pit of my pain, the Lord revealed a need and vision to serve. My pain, His gain.

I pray this study is a safe and an encouraging place to walk out your pain, where grief, fear, and doubt are countered with hope, patience, and prayer. No matter your pain, loss, or experience, we are all connected in Christ. Whatever you may be dealing with, fighting for, or walking through—you are not alone.

With love,

Nicole

*"I am the Lord!
There is nothing
too difficult for me.
I'll come back next
year at the time
I promised, and
Sarah will already
have a son."*

Genesis 18:14, NIV

Sarah

{Stephanie Hanrahan}

There is perhaps no woman in the Bible as familiar with the waiting game as Sarah. Her greatest desires didn't come easily for her, nor did they come on her timetable. But somewhere throughout the story of her life, Sarah was able to turn her impatience into obedience—and the outcome of that small shift would change generations to come.

It has been said that Sarah, wife to Abraham, was a beautiful woman. She held the pretty card, and even pharaohs and kings were quick to take note. This worried her husband, and when they traveled to Egypt, Abraham instructed Sarah to say she was his sister so that his life may be spared on the account of her beauty (Genesis 12:11–13).

Abraham was justified in his thinking, as Sarah was taken into Pharaoh's harem, where she was adorned, admired, and protected until the truth eventually came out, and they were commanded to leave Egypt.

Ten years after returning to their homeland, Sarah and Abraham were still childless. As Sarah's impatience mounted, she turned to her handmaid, Hagar, and suggested she birth a baby with Abraham.

But this was never the way God intended for Sarah and Abraham's lineage to continue, and because Sarah decided on disobedience instead of following God's discernment, consequences were to come.

After Hagar gave birth to Abraham's son, Ishmael, stress entered their household, and Sarah's authority was no longer respected. As she turned back to God for guidance, Sarah realized her impatience had led her to act unfaithfully. God had promised to bless Sarah and Abraham with a baby boy (Genesis 17), but by taking matters into their own hands, they had not acted as God willed.

Finally, at ninety years old, God again promised Sarah a son. Well past childbearing years, Sarah laughed. God asked Abraham, "Why did Sarah laugh, saying, 'Shall I surely bear a child, since I am old?'" (Genesis 18:13, NKJV). God responded to Sarah's doubts in a profound way:

"Is there anything too difficult for the Lord?"

In spite of her initial laughter, Sarah came to truly believe God would do what he said, and at the age of 91, Sarah birthed her long-awaited baby boy, Isaac. Her laughter then changed to that of pure joy and endless worship, as she became not only mother to one son but mother to many nations due to her diligence, trust, and faithfulness in God's unseen plan.

truths

How easy is it to take control of situations instead of consulting God first? How common is it to grow impatient during the wait, thinking God has forgotten you and your greatest needs? Sarah fell victim to both of these circumstances, and so have I.

After years of abusive and destructive relationships, I had finally met and married a man of such worth. Much like Sarah, I thought life held a linear path that I was happy to follow: find man, make baby. After all, there was no greater need in my heart than to become a mother.

But that was my plan, not God's. First came two miscarriages, accompanied by heartache, pain, loss of hope, and of course, waiting. Then, after my children were born, I was once again called to adjust my sails when I learned they both had special needs (autism). The idea I had in my head, the children I conjured up, were not the ones God intended. Like Sarah, I had to mourn what I thought life would look like and trust that God would bless me with an even greater plan.

Patience and perseverance are key qualities when trusting God. Sometimes my fear of what my children will become or how much pain they will endure consumes me. When you have periods of no progress, it's very easy to get discouraged. But Sarah was almost one hundred (one hundred!) before she received the outcome she wanted. If she was faithful during the wait, then we can be too. For what sustains us is hope. We must always remain pregnant with possibility.

From Sarah's son Isaac came countless multitudes of nations and kings. Sarah's faith had a long-lasting impact on the world—and so we must follow her great example.

Whatever you are waiting for will reap a bigger gift than you could ever imagine. God is good like that. He changes our doubt to diligence—our pain into our pulpit.

Remember, there's nothing too difficult for Him to overcome.

questions

» What are you waiting for? How long has this desire been on your heart? Instead of taking matters into your own hands, what are some active steps you can take to turn it over to God?

» Describe a time you've questioned God's plan for you. Did you act with human effort (i.e., when Sarah elicited Hagar's help to have a baby), or remain patient and prayerful?

» Think of a time you laughed at what God was calling you to do. Did you follow his lead anyway? If not, knowing that, just like with Sarah, it's never too late, how can you act now to fulfill His call?

digging deeper

"He has made everything beautiful in its time. He has also set eternity in the human heart; yet no one can fathom what God has done from beginning to end" (Ecclesiastes 3:11, NIV).

Knowing God's word draws us closer to Him. Read, meditate, and obey are the commands our Father gave Joshua. Read the scripture above. Meditate on how this applies to your life today. Is God asking you to be obedient in the wait? Write out a prayer to Him, surrendering your ways to Him.

prayer

"Father, you are a God that never gives up. You never give up on us. You never give up on your plans for us. You have created us in your image: whole, perfect, and capable. Allow us to surrender to the wait. To remain faithful instead of frightened. To know that whatever the end result will be, it is your will. Let us laugh in the face of fear and know the road ahead has already been blessed by you." Amen.

"Isaac prayed to the Lord on behalf of his wife, because she was childless. The Lord answered his prayer, and his wife Rebekah became pregnant."

Genesis 25:21, NIV

Rebekah

{Lisbeth Van Daalen}

Rebekah was a descendant of Abraham's brother. When it came time for Abraham's son Isaac to be married, Abraham sent his servant out of Canaan and into his homeland Nahor to find his son a suitable wife. Genesis Chapter 24 tells of Rebekah's act of kindness and generosity that divinely led to Abrahams's servant finding and selecting her as Isaac's wife.

After Rebekah and her family agreed that she should marry Isaac, we learn of her obedience and bravery as she follows the servant to marry her husband. Rebekah follows the servant, a stranger to her, into a foreign land she's never seen to marry a man she has never met. Even when her family requests extra time with her, she bravely presses onward to her new life with Isaac. The two meet and are married, as Genesis 24:67 says, Isaac "loved her" and "was comforted."

Rebekah and Isaac were married for twenty years before becoming parents. During this time, scripture says that Rebekah was childless and that Isaac prayed on her behalf. After 20 years together, a set of twin boys joined their family. An answered prayer! During her pregnancy, the Old Testament reads that Rebekah asked the Lord why there was such a jostling inside her belly. When the time comes for her to give birth, she has twins, Esau and Jacob. This pregnancy is just the beginning of a dramatic and crucially important storyline that leads to the twelve tribes of Israel. Genesis Chapters 26–28 tell more about Rebekah's part in her sons' story.

truths

Although the scripture readings on what Rebekah's life was like before her pregnancy are short, they speak volumes about the kind of faith this woman of God and her husband had. Particularly in the beginning of her life, her obedience strikes me. She is a young woman brought to marry a distant cousin in a land that is not her home. We are left to guess if it was her sense of adventure and gusto that led to her confidence in the servant or if it was simply obedience and trust in God. I have to believe that to make such a bold choice, it was at least in part the latter. She was certainly rewarded upon meeting Isaac, who we know loved her, was comforted by her, and later prayed over her. Her ability to trust and seek a new life in the unknown led to great blessings.

Genesis Chapter 25 mentions that Isaac is 40 years old when he marries Rebekah and later says that he is 60 years old when his twin sons are born. While we don't know exactly when during that 20-year span of marriage Isaac prayed for his wife, you can be sure it was a very long time to wait upon the Lord.

As Rebekah grew older, being childless and married to Isaac, who had a great prophecy spoken over his life, would have been extremely difficult. It must have felt like a hopeless situation. Those that have endured the pain of infertility or infant loss know the heartbreak that comes with each passing year your family doesn't look the way you envisioned. Has God forsaken the plan you once felt confident he planted in your heart? Imagining that mindset for twenty years is a dire state. Rebekah's faith and resolve must have been strong. We don't hear stories of her resorting to a second wife or other shortcuts to motherhood, like many of the women in the Old Testament did when they were barren.

Instead, we hear that her husband prays on her behalf. I love the image of this great man, over 40 years old, the son of mighty Abraham, asking God to please open his wife's womb. There are so many reactions that Isaac and Rebekah could have had to twenty years of childlessness. The fact that God chose to write a story deeply impacted by PRAYER is not a mistake. While patience was required, God shows through this story the great love He has for us.

There's a lot to read between the lines here – God's weeping alongside them as they waited and His perfect plan moving into motion as he sent twins to fill Rebekah's womb. After Isaac prayed, THE LORD ANSWERED his prayer. Those are beautiful words. Rebekah likely wondered when or if that prayer would ever be answered. But double the blessing arrives!

The last story we are told before Rebekah embarks on her journey of parenting twin sons is that of a jostling in her belly.

She actually cries out and questions the Lord, asking why is this happening to me. I relate so much to her candor and confusion in this moment. She has finally been given the pregnancy that she and Isaac have prayed for, but her pregnancy is not what she expected. So often in life, I find myself praying and waiting upon the Lord, striving to be trusting and steadfast in prayer, and rejoicing when I'm granted the desires of my heart! But I often find myself questioning the Lord, even after I've been blessed. It's easy to feel shame or guilt when we question the Lord about a blessing, in this case, about a precious baby! But it's important to remember that He is our Abba Father. He longs for us to come to Him with questions, fears, and concerns, just as Rebekah did. His plan for our lives doesn't end when a prayer is answered; instead, the conversation continues because we need our Father's guidance, even in blessings.

questions

» When has an act of obedience led to blessings in your life?

- » Who is praying for you right now? How has that prayer impacted you? Who else could you reach out to for prayer during this season?

- » Do you pray with your spouse, family members, or friends? Are you able to ask them for prayer? How can you open up that communication? Could Rebekah and Isaac's story prompt a conversation?

» Do you find yourself afraid to question God or constantly questioning His plans? Do you feel comfortable seeking answers or bringing forth fears to God, even in a situation you may consider to be a blessing?

digging deeper

Jesus has but one request, follow Me. The way He prays to His Father while here on earth gives us a guideline to do the same. In breaking down the prayers Jesus offers to the Lord, He follows a similar pattern.

Are you stuck in your prayer life, not sure how to build your relationship with our Father? Here's a quick acronym to follow, "A.C.T. S.." Remember, God doesn't want your words, He wants you.

Adoration: Give God praise and honor for who He is as Lord over all.

Confession: Honestly deal with your sin in your prayer life.

Thanksgiving: Verbalize what you're grateful for in your life and in the world around you.

Supplication: Pray for the needs of others and yourself.

prayer

Lord, there is so much I can learn from Rebekah's story; it tells me how being obedient and steadfast in prayer can bring me closer to You. God, increase my patience as I wait on Your timing. Direct my heart towards obedience even when life feels unknown. Give my husband, friends, and family strength to love me and pray for me through these trials. Above all, Lord, let my desires, fears, and questions always be brought to your feet. Amen.

"Then God remembered Rachel. He listened to her and opened her womb."

Genesis 30: 22, CSB

Rachel

{Sara Blakeney}

Rachel was a woman who waited a long time for her dreams to come true. Like Rebekah and Sarah, she was unable to have children, and the longsuffering of her barrenness made her feel abandoned and forgotten by God. But God remembered Rachel, and in His timing, He opened her womb. He gave her children and ensured the lineage of the Israelite people, just as He promised many generations before.

It seemed like Rachel had to wait for everything important in her life. She waited seven years to marry the man she loved, Jacob. He was smitten the first time he laid eyes on her. She was "lovely in form and beautiful," the whole package. Jacob asked Rachel's father, Laban, for her hand in marriage, and Laban agreed under one condition: that Jacob first work for him for seven years. Jacob complied, and Rachel waited.

At the end of seven years. Rachel, no doubt, was eager to start her new life with Jacob. However, in an audacious act of cunning on the wedding night, Laban gave Rachel's sister Leah to Jacob instead. He snuck her into the wedding tent, and Jacob didn't notice until it was too late.

Thanks to this bait-and-switch, Rachel again found herself waiting. Seven more years, to be exact.

We have two sisters who are married to the same man by means of deception. Rachel and Leah were constantly at each other's throats. While Rachel was beautiful, Leah was said to have "weak eyes," which is the Old Testament way of saying she had "a great personality." Although Rachel and Jacob were madly in love, Rachel was barren. Meanwhile, Leah gave birth to four sons in rapid succession. Leah's robust fertility was a source of great jealousy for Rachel. I can only imagine the scene: Leah having to endure Jacob's love for Rachel and Rachel having to watch four little boys run around Leah, climb into her lap, and hug her neck.

Finally, Rachel couldn't take anymore. The jealousy toward her sister, combined with the emptiness of barrenness, culminated in a breaking point of desperation. Her anguish boiled over, and she lashed out at Jacob, "Give me children, or I'll die!" (Genesis 30:1, NIV).

Reading those words even today, one can feel the gut-wrenching pain. Rachel had reached the end of her rope and suffocated in her hopelessness; she didn't want to go on living. Jacob, who seemed to have reached a breaking point of his own, angrily replied, "Am I in the place of God, who has kept you from having children?" (Genesis 30:2, NIV).

I wish I could tell you that this breaking point was the end of the waiting for Rachel and that she was able to conceive. Unfortunately, her barrenness persisted, and the waiting continued.

Figuring that God had forgotten her, she took matters into her own hands. She gave her maidservant to Jacob as a surrogate. Sound familiar? The maidservant had two sons, which Rachel adopted as her own.

Not to be outdone, Leah gave her maidservant to Jacob too, who also bore two sons. In case you're keeping score, that's two children for Rachel and six for Leah.

Rachel had a backup plan. She discovered that one of Leah's sons was in possession of some mandrakes, an herb rumored to enhance fertility. So, she struck a deal with Leah, trading the mandrakes for a night of passion with Jacob. Leah agreed and, of course, conceived again. And then again.

Meanwhile, the mandrakes didn't seem to work for Rachel, and she remained barren. The plan had backfired. It seemed like Rachel would forever be childless.

One day, Rachel's dream finally came true, "Then God remembered Rachel. He listened to her and opened her womb" (Genesis 30:22, CSB). At first glance, it seems like God had forgotten all about Rachel and then suddenly "remembered" her. But that's not what the word remembered means here. It is the Hebrew word *zakar*, which translates as "to turn one's attention to someone and act on their behalf."[1]

---

1 "When The Bible says God remembered something, what does that mean?" Compelling Truth. https://www.compellingtruth.org/God-remembered.html

God had never forgotten Rachel; He was simply waiting for the perfect time to act on her behalf. Her waiting was finally over! She conceived and gave birth to a son whom she named Joseph.

She eventually had another son named Benjamin. All in all, Leah and Rachel had twelve children, who became the twelve tribes of Israel.

truths

I can relate to Rachel's suffering. I, too have been waiting for children for a long, long time. I have watched women around me get pregnant easily, their lives full and happy as mothers. Meanwhile, I dream of days filled with tiny voices calling me "Mommy" and the "pitter-patter of little feet." My painful reality is an echoing silence in an empty house. And it echoes the emptiness in my heart.

Like Rachel, for years, I had tried everything: medical tests, fertility treatments, herbal remedies, you name it. And still my womb – and my heart – remained empty. As one's hope begins to wear down to a nub, it's hard not to feel forgotten by God. God, don't you see me? God, don't you care? There were days when the pain of childlessness was all-consuming, and I wondered how I could go on living in this excruciating state of waiting.

Like Rachel, I felt forgotten by God. But here's where my story takes a different turn from hers. I had people in my life with whom I could share these dark thoughts, people who were trustworthy and who knew the truth about God's Word. They gently challenged my beliefs. They showed me that all the self-talk, that I was incomplete without children, was a lie.

They reminded me that through my relationship with Jesus, I can enjoy an abundant life, a life full of purpose in Him. Honestly, it sounded too good to be true. But I decided to give it a try. I turned to God. Instead of my usual litany of blaming Him, pleading with Him, and reviewing my resume of pain with Him, I simply asked to be able to find my completeness and purpose in Him.

It was in that moment that I discovered the truth: God had not forgotten me; on the contrary, God "is near to the brokenhearted and saves those who are crushed in spirit" (Psalm 34:18, NASB).

As I spent time with Him, I discovered the greatest intimacy I have ever known. It began to fill the empty place left by my childlessness and dislodge the bitterness of my grieving heart.

Over time, this sweet place with the Lord became my reason for living. I looked forward to my time with Him because I knew that the emptiness would be filled with joy and hope in His presence. I was not forgotten; God remembered me and acted on my behalf by filling me with abundant life. I feel like I've discovered a secret – or more like a secret place, a hidden garden or an inner room. It is a place I can run to, meet with my God, and find all the joy and purpose I need.

My story isn't over yet. He may remember me with children one day. When He does, they will be a joyful addition to my already joy-full life. But even if He doesn't, I will not feel as though I will die. God has remembered me. I have found my life in Him, and nothing or no one can ever take it from me.

questions

» How do you relate to Rachel's story?

» How have your issues related to children affected your relationship with those closest to you?

» Have you ever felt like your grief has been all-consuming? Have you ever felt like you couldn't go on?

» Do you have others in your life with whom you can share your deepest thoughts and feelings? Are they able to help you identify where you are off base in your beliefs about yourself and God?

» What would it look like for God to remember you in your current circumstances?

» Are you open to finding your purpose in Christ alone and letting Him lead you to that special place of intimate relationship with Him?

digging deeper

Scripture frequently speaks about God remembering His people. He remembered Noah in the flood (Genesis 8:1), Abraham and his prayers (Genesis 19:29), Hannah in her barrenness (1 Samuel 1:19), and the Israelite people in their bondage (Exodus 2:24). In each instance, God acted on behalf of His people. What does that mean for us today?

Jesus said that he came so that we could have an abundant life (John 10:10). What does that mean? Is there a difference between an abundant life and a trouble-free life?

prayer

Dear Lord, thank you that you are a God who is close to the brokenhearted. Thank you that in your great love, you choose to remember me in my pain and act on my behalf. Help me to press in and discover the secret place of intimacy with you that will give me a joy and purpose that I have not known before. Jesus, I thank you that your promise to me is an abundant life in you. Amen.

"And behold, your relative Elizabeth in her old age has also conceived a son, and this is the sixth month with her who was called barren. For nothing will be impossible with God."

Luke 1:36–37, ESV

Elizabeth

{Anitha Thomas Abraham}

In the backdrop of the coming of the Messiah was another miraculous birth. The story is told of Zechariah and Elizabeth, a godly couple who, according to Luke, was “advanced in years” (Luke 1:6). Other translations aren't so graciously worded...essentially, they were “very old.”

This is especially significant because they were barren. Or so they thought.

One day, while Zechariah was performing his priestly duties, he had a divine visitation with a proclamation: he would soon have a son. Unfortunately for Zechariah, this was a bit too much to handle, so he began questioning the angel. His lack of faith resulted in a lack of words - God silenced him until the prophecy came to pass.

Elizabeth received the news but chose to remain hidden for the first five months. When she received a visit from Mary, she rejoiced in seeing the soon-to-be mother of the long-awaited Messiah.

“Now the time came...” and John was born.

The people celebrated with her, and when it was time for the baby's circumcision, Elizabeth declared just as they had been told, "...he shall be called John" (Luke 1:60).

The people disputed this due to the traditional way of naming children, but Zechariah confirmed this by writing it on a tablet. Then, at that point, he was able to speak again and began to prophesy over his son.

Elizabeth's story ends with, "And the child grew and became strong in spirit, and he was in the wilderness until the day of his public appearance to Israel" (Luke 1:80, ESV).

truths

Most of us have a dream. Something we want to see happen in our lives.

For some, it is buying a certain car or a house in a particular neighborhood. For others, it is a dream job or fairy tale wedding. Ask around, and you will probably hear something unique from each person.

Depending on the season of life I was in, my dreams have varied. When I was a kid, I wanted to be a recording artist (my hairbrush doubled as a microphone). As I got older, I still enjoyed singing but felt like God was calling me out of my comfort zone.

Eventually, I started a blog and a women's Bible study group. I began having dreams of what could be for us as a group and for me as a writer and teacher.

For years, those dreams were just that...dreams.

No speaking invitations, just me teaching my small group. Sometimes 20 people would show up... sometimes 2.

No publishers, just me writing my weekly posts. Sometimes, thousands would engage; sometimes, it seemed like only my immediate family were interested in what I had to say.

For years, it was just me trying to be faithful to what I knew God called me to do.

Then, it happened.

What I had been hoping for, dreaming of, and praying about finally happened. I was asked to speak at a women's conference. Then, that same week, I was asked to speak at another event. I was blown away. What was God up to?

I traced my steps. Surely, I had done something to finally cause this to happen? Or did I say something differently when I prayed?

I couldn't come up with anything.

It seems that Elizabeth had her own dream-come-true moment. Can you imagine how she felt when Zechariah shared the news of his visit with an angel? What went through her mind?

Beyond the excitement, was there a "why now" moment? Why did God decide this was the right time to give them a child? Maybe she traced her steps to see if she had done anything differently. Had she been a little nicer to Zechariah that week? Is it because she spent less time chatting with the other ladies at, He-brews (the local coffee shop) and more time at the temple?

The more we read, the more we know. The birth of John the Baptist was bigger than Zechariah and Elizabeth. In fact, it was bigger than John the Baptist himself.

When the right time came, God sent his Son (Galatians 4:4). The timing of Jesus' arrival was a factor in God's plan. That means so was the birth of John. After all, it was prophesied that John would prepare the way of the Messiah.

Maybe you are a Christ follower who is doing everything right that you know to do...and like Elizabeth, there is a BUT in your story, too.

Single. Childless. Diagnosed. Unemployed. Bankrupt. Unfulfilled dream.

Elizabeth's story reminds us that our promise may not be fulfilled how or when we expect. In the meantime, we remain submitted to God and His plan... and keep doing what we've always done.

We pray. We wait. We hope. We believe.

Her story also reminds us that sometimes what we've believed for may just be waiting on the right time to come.

And in His time, we see: “Blessed is she who has believed that the Lord would fulfill his promises to her!” (Luke 1:45).

questions

» What dream have you put on the shelf? Why?

» When something seems impossible, what is your first response?

» Looking back on your life, when has God's timing been different from yours? What did you learn in the process?

digging deeper

What is the common thread between Elizabeth, Abraham, Joseph, and Hannah?

They were all believing for something... and had to wait to see it fulfilled. There are typically two reasons why we have to wait on what we believe God has promised us.

1. For our growth—a baby who is born prematurely may look like a baby, but that doesn't mean he or she has fully developed. There is still a lot of growth that has to happen on the inside for them to be ready for their arrival into the outside world. Depending on our situation, the same could be true of us. "Until the time came to fulfill his dreams, the LORD tested Joseph's character" (Psalm 105:19).

2. For His time—that sounds like a cliche Christian answer, but it is a powerful truth. Sometimes, our waiting has nothing to do with us and everything to do with God. Galatians 4:4 says that Jesus came at the "right" time. To everything, there is a time, season, and purpose. There is a perfect, God-ordained time for the desires of your heart to be fulfilled and also a purpose in the waiting.

While you wait, may I encourage you in this? Pray (so God can do what only He can do), Position Yourself (do what you can to get where you want to be!), and Pursue Life Now (live out everything God has for you in this season).

prayer

Dear God, I am thankful that my life is in Your sovereign hands. I know that Your timing is perfect, but sometimes it is hard to wait. There are dreams that You have put in my heart. Help me to remember that Your ways are higher than mine. Give me peace as I wait. Thank You for orchestrating everything for my good and Your glory. In the name of Jesus Christ, I pray. Amen.

"And she made a vow, saying, 'LORD Almighty, if you will only look on your servant's misery and remember me, and not forget your servant but give her a son, then I will give him to the LORD for all the days of his life, and no razor will ever be used on his head.'"

1 Samuel 1:11, NIV

Hannah

{Becky Bierwas}

We know Hannah for her sorrow. She was married to Elkanah, who also had another wife, Peninnah. Peninnah had children, but Hannah did not. Hannah longed for a son but could not have children. Year after year, she would travel with Elkanah and Peninnah (all her children in tow) to worship the Lord at Shiloh.

Elkanah would give portions of his sacrifice to both of his wives, reserving more for Hannah "because he loved her, and the Lord had closed her womb" (1 Samuel 1:5, NIV). The years of travel, all while remaining barren, were difficult for Hannah as she faced the constant torment of Peninnah.

Peninnah's children were a reminder of her perceived shortcomings, her unwavering desire, and her unanswered prayers. Yet, Hannah persevered.

As a woman struggling with infertility, she not only responded to Peninnah's personal taunts and jabs with grace and/or no response at all, but she accepted God's promise with unwavering faith.

In her faithfulness, Hannah walked into the Lord's temple and poured out her soul to God. When Eli, the high priest, witnessed her conversation with God, he thought Hannah was drunk. "'Not so, my lord,' Hannah replied. 'I am a woman who is deeply troubled. I have not been drinking wine or beer; I was pouring out my soul to the Lord. Do not take your servant for a wicked woman; I have been praying here out of my great anguish and grief'" (1 Samuel 1:15–16, NIV).

How often, in the midst of deep grief, might someone mistake our outcries and pleas with the Lord as intoxication? It doesn't stand too far from the truth because the truth is we are intoxicated with so much love and grief. We pray for the children that never come, for those that have not come yet, and for those who did come and are now being held in the arms of Jesus; a reunion we long for with every fiber of our being, every minute of every day.

After pouring out her soul to God, Hannah left the temple, and her face was glowing. She stood before God and made a vow with Him. A vow that would bring her a son. A son that she would, in turn, dedicate to the Lord for his entire life.

A prayer that started from a heart of bitterness ended in unwavering faith and trust in the Lord. A faith that undoubtedly believed in God's plan for her life: a trust that had healing qualities, her appetite restored, and her face glowing. God heard Hannah, and He granted her a son, whom she named Samuel; saying, "Because I asked the Lord for him" (1 Samuel 1:20, NIV)

When Hannah weaned Samuel, she returned to Shiloh and stood before Eli. "'Pardon me, my lord. As surely as you live, I am the woman who stood here beside you praying to the Lord. I prayed for this child, and the Lord has granted me what I asked of him. So now I give him to the Lord. For his whole life he will be given over to the Lord.' And he worshiped the Lord there" (1 Samuel 1:26–27, NIV).

God's faithfulness brought Hannah full circle, a promise kept on both ends. She left her only-born son that day to be raised up by Eli, the high priest. She dedicated his life, and her own, to God's will. She surrendered to His greater plan trusting His story in her life was bigger and better than what she could ever possibly understand. To have the faith of Hannah, Jesus, help us all.

truths

The God that Hannah so faithfully cried out to is the same God that has called my two babies home. They're resting in the arms of Jesus; my arms left empty with a longing to hold them.

As a career nanny, I am forever thankful for the opportunity to raise up little ones but nonetheless have a longing desire for my own; being a nanny just isn't the same. I yearn to be a mama. I knew from a young age I was born to be a mother. The ache and pull on my heart started right after college. It wasn't until I turned 33 that I brought my pain and desire to the Lord. With open hands, I said, "Your will be done." I surrendered. I was tired from the continual craving, the hurt in my heart, and the back and forth inside my head.

One month after my full surrender, my youngest son, Rhys, was conceived. My prayerful cries and daily wrestling with the Lord were heard. My story starts out much like Hannah's. Promises, bargains, and the intoxicating depth of my desires left at the feet of Jesus and His will. Oh, how humbled I was with the gift and blessing that came with my new title, Mama.

I was so incredibly connected to my son the entire pregnancy. My fondest memory with Rhys, in utero, was going to church on Sundays. I would stand, belt out worship songs, have an intimate moment with God, and rub my belly; the only way I could hold my son at the time. The depth of the love I felt for my son, and for God, in those exact moments was so incredibly special and will forever be cherished.

Six days before my due date, at three o'clock in the morning, on July 23, 2017, Rhys was called home. His beating heart rested, his soul received by the arms of Jesus. Two days later, I delivered Rhys. His almost 10-pound perfect body lay in my trembling arms, our only meeting here earth side. I have no answers as to why he passed or why his time here with me was so short.

Why, after complete submission to God and His will, am I still alone? The greatest desire of my heart was given and is now gone.

I feel like Hannah, at times, living in a world full of Peninnahs, a single bereaved mother dealing with taunting and daily reminders that I have no living children. There are days that are so heavy it feels like I am suffocating under the weight of my reality. My heart grieves for my babies and, simultaneously, the waiting in the unknown. I'm back to where I was at 33, but worse.

I am a mama, though this is invisible to those around me. I've felt the weight of this word in every sense through new life and abrupt loss. Still, working as a nanny, I happily care for others' babies, and yet behind closed doors, I'm forced to wait. With a barren home and womb, my heart yearns for more children. I was born with the heart of a mother, have been bestowed the honor, and yet, still, here I am, alone, waiting. It's excruciating most days.

Like Hannah, from an early age, God placed a longing desire in my heart to be a mother. It is difficult for most to understand and just as difficult for me to be "content." That aspect of my life has yet to be fulfilled. My heart and hope are that I can embody a little more of Hannah in the midst of the wait, responding with grace, or not at all, to the jabs and taunts of my reality. I want to know and have faith in the God that gives and takes away. He has formed me and my desires. He has my happy ending in mind.

God knows my heart, hears my cries, and will continue to sit with me in the heartache and hopelessness. He will stay until it is redeemed. Proverbs 13:12 says, "Hope deferred makes the heart sick" (NIV). I continue to do my best to keep the faith and hope for more children.

I lean into God and His will and continue to glorify Him through my pain, my ache, my desires, and my tears.

God worked in Hannah's life. He used her story of sorrow to display His everlasting love and faithfulness. She turned to Him in deep pain. And then, Samuel. Surrendering Samuel back to the Lord is evidence of God's work in Hannah's life.

Even amongst sorrow and great grief, God was working. Hannah's tears were a beautiful part of the story God was writing for Israel. Tears, sorrow, and heartache are woven amongst her personal story to write an even bigger story, all the while bringing glory to God.

There is not enough time to adequately describe what the journey of losing a child entails, let alone the journey of waiting for the child(ren) you so desperately pray for and still do not have. My hope in sharing and relating to Hannah is not to take away from either of our stories. I'm obediently sharing the incredibly rough and ugly parts of God's big story that is still playing out in my life. My heart is simply to share with you that I have been angry, so deeply sad, hopeless, and at times wished to be in the same place as my babies. I have struggled with moving forward, with the Peninnah moments, with the exhaustive injustice of my reality.

Even then, even in the mess, God has continued to pursue me. He has spoken to me and pushed through my walls. He meets me where I am. These are the moments I want for you—the ones I cling to, the ones that carried me through, the moments that have become my own personal Shiloh. Lean in, meet God, pour out your heart, and lay down your sorrow. At times, my cries didn't utter a sound, much like Hannah's.

Grief is intoxicating. It makes us do crazy things, our love howling to the world. Jesus, be near and encourage us as we wait, hope, and trust in your perfect timing.

questions

» When life feels hopeless and it's difficult to trust God's faithfulness and promises, what can you do to regain your "glow"?

» Hannah responded to taunting with grace or, even harder, not at all. How can this be your response when those around you don't understand your yearning, sorrow, or grief?

» Would you be able to leave your firstborn child at a temple to serve God for the entirety of their life? Let the thought of this resonate; God did the same. Hannah sacrificing and surrendering her son mirrors the story of Christ, God giving and surrendering His son. This, my friends, is how much He loves us. I can't imagine doing as Hannah did, and I imagine God grieved for His son too. God sees us, and He knows our pain. How can your heart soften towards God, knowing His big story is our best future?

» God values prayer. It is our direct line of communication with Him. God invites us to wrestle with him in prayer, to pour out our deepest desires, questions, and tears. What are some ways you have wrestled with God and/or what do you need to surrender to Him in prayer?

digging deeper

Hannah's story of infertility and surrender/sacrifice is one of many. "By faith Abraham's wife Sarah became fertile long after menopause because she believed God would be faithful to His promise" (Hebrews 11:11, VOICE). At age 90, Sarah conceived and gave birth to Isaac. Read Genesis 21:1–18. What does this verse show us when it comes to trusting God and His timing?

Abraham and Sarah waited more than 25 years for God's promise to come to fruition. Even then, God asked Abraham to take Isaac and offer him as a burnt sacrifice. Read Genesis 22:1–18. What does this passage reveal to us about Abraham's heart? How does Abraham's act of trust show his faith in God?

Let's not forget the ultimate sacrifice; God sent his only son Jesus as a sacrifice for us all. He knows the pain of separation, the heartache of letting go. "For God so loved the world that he gave his one and only Son, that whoever believes in him shall not perish but have eternal life" (John 3:16). What life can God provide as we meditate on his own sacrifice for us? How can we apply it to our own journeys, struggles and emotions when it comes to infertility and child loss?

Can you see the connection between the Old Testament stories of infertility and sacrifice and the New Testament story of sacrifice? How do you think each story leads up to God's big story of redemption? What is God speaking to you through each of these stories?

God's sacrifice lends to His personality. He can relate to us in our time of sorrow, pain, and separation. He, too, offered his Son for our lives. How does this change your heart toward our God?

Hannah not only gave birth to Samuel, but her womb became fertile. May we trust in the Lord with everything. He is able to bless abundantly and does so beyond imagination. He is sovereign, closing and opening our wombs. He is beside us amongst the deepest grief, sorrow, and loss. There is kindness in God's refusal.

His ways are better than our ways. His timing is perfect. Even when we fail to trust, He mourns each and every loss with us. He captures and bottles each tear, holding them close. While this is, at times, so incredibly difficult to grasp, my prayer is that we can allow our hearts to soften; soften enough to accept this truth. We need not dismiss our emotions or justify the pain or loss but instead allow ourselves to wait in expectation of God's redemption.

prayer

Lord, some of us may be coming to You in bitterness like Hannah did. We are broken and hopeless, anguished and downcast. We ask, Lord, for You to honor and accept these emotions. We lay our deep grief at your feet. Extend favor to us, fill us with hope and faith, and continue to surround us with those who will encourage us and point us to You.

Lead us to your truths, your promises, and your faithfulness. God, may our faith remain as strong as Hannah's. May we wait expectantly for You to fulfill our heart's desires, as she did. May we trust that You hear our hearts and feel our pain. May we live a life of hope, each breath declaring your goodness and faithfulness. On the days we can't, Lord, surround us with those like Eli who will lift us to You. It is in Your holy and blessed name we pray. Amen.

"One day Elisha went to Shunem. And a well-to-do woman was there, who urged him to stay for a meal. So whenever he came by, he stopped there to eat. She said to her husband, "I know that this man who often comes our way is a holy man of God. Let's make a small room on the roof and put in it a bed and a table, a chair and a lamp for him. Then he can stay there whenever he comes to us."

2 Kings 4: 8–10, NIV

Shunammite Woman

Part 1: "don't lie to me"

{Lindsey Jensen}

Tucked inside the Old Testament, there are a few pages dedicated to a woman and her incredible story. The scriptures call her "the Shunammite woman." We are never told her name.

But she is undoubtedly real—a woman with a heartbeat, skin, good and bad hair days, feelings, experiences—and her story was saved through the centuries to teach us something. The scriptures immediately define her as "notable" or "well-to-do."

We find out that she is married and lives in a home where the prophet Elisha routinely passes by on his journey from Mount Carmel to Shunem (or surrounding areas).

Each time he and his servant, Gehazi, would pass by, she would prepare them a meal. One day she asks her husband if they can build a room for Elisha so that he can have a place to rest. So, they do.

From just this much of her story, we can infer some things about her. It is clear that she is very giving and generous. She is respectful of her husband (ya know, discussing the whole "Fixer Upper" idea with him before knocking down walls). They have the means to build on to their home. She believes Elisha is a Holy Man of God and respects him. The Shunammite woman has faith in God and the men He is using to do His work. Let's read more.

> One day when Elisha came, he went up to his room and lay down there. He said to his servant Gehazi, "Call the Shunammite." So he called her, and she stood before him. Elisha said to him, "Tell her, 'You have gone to all this trouble for us. Now what can be done for you? Can we speak on your behalf to the king or the commander of the army?'"
>
> She replied, "I have a home among my own people."
>
> "What can be done for her?" Elisha asked.
>
> Gehazi said, "She has no son, and her husband is old."
>
> Then Elisha said, "Call her." So he called her, and she stood in the doorway. "About this time next year," Elisha said, "you will hold a son in your arms."

Wait for it...

> "No, my lord!" she objected. "Please, man of God, don't mislead your servant!" (2 Kings 4:11-16, NIV).

I can hear the pin drop. Can you feel her pain?

She has buried the longing for a child deep within her heart, hoping that she can leave it there for fear that this dream has died. We don't know all the details of this story; how long had they tried to have children? Had she conceived and lost a child? Had she married later in life and was older? How many prayers were spoken asking God for a child? How many tears were shed when they went unanswered? We simply don't know. What we do know is that she has remained faithful to God and loved others well despite this. But somewhere along the way, she has lost hope in this dream, and the very thought of hoping for it hurts. The mention of this unfulfilled longing hits a nerve, and she cannot hide her pain, nor can she hold her tongue.

What you need to understand about this time period is that everything is very proper, and there were strict rules with prophets. Until this moment, we can assume that any conversation she had with Elisha was through his servant. It was not proper for Elisha to speak directly to her or vice versa. When we consider this, we see that she responds directly to Elisha (the man of God) and, for a moment, disregards the rules of religion.

truths

There is so much to take from the beginning of this story. The quick "I have everything I need" response she gives when they ask what can be done for her. How many times does someone say, "How are you?" or "What can I do for you?" and you quickly reply with "I'm fine," "all good," or "I don't need anything." Even in some of the hardest seasons of my life, I have replied just as she does.

I think our world tells us that we have to be strong and independent; we shouldn't need anything or anyone. Or maybe it's pride. Maybe we don't want to admit that we are struggling. Or maybe we don't want to share this struggle again because it feels as if we are a burden to those around us. Can you relate to the raw emotion attached to her unfulfilled dreams?

How about the ache of disappointment in life that she has covered up and attempted to forget? Don't we all have these in some form or another? Whether it is a desire that never came to fruition or a dream that seemed perfect but became a nightmare. Is it a failed marriage or an empty womb? A prodigal child? An empty ring finger? A betrayal? A disease? A death?

I am so thankful that God's promises don't rely on my perfect faith. I am sure our un-named Shunammite woman felt the same way. She gets upset at the very mention of this unfulfilled longing. She can't bear to be disappointed again. It is better left buried. She has faith in God, but she just can't believe for this.

I can relate. I never imagined I would be in my early 40's, unmarried and without children. The pain of this unmet longing is so piercing at times that the very mention of hope in this circumstance stings.

I understand her response to Elisha and her desire to just hide those longings deep within. But after the Shunammite woman so honestly cries out, "Do not lie to me!" the very next verse says, "But the woman became pregnant, and the next year about that same time she gave birth to a son, just as Elisha had told her" (2 Kings 4:17, NIV).

Grace. Once again, His grace comes in and sweeps over the moments when our faith is low and reminds us although our faith wavers, His faithfulness does not.

questions

» What part of her story is relatable to you?

» Why do you think she replied to Elijah with "I am just fine" instead of taking him up on his offer to do something for her?

» Have you ever had an unmet longing that you buried deep within? If so, I encourage you to share that with the Lord.

digging deeper

Sometimes we don't understand God's timing, but it is always perfect. Read 1 Samuel 1:10–11 to find a story of a girl crying out to God. A girl who was waiting for an unmet longing. Then read 1 Samuel 3:19–21 to see the importance God saw in the timing of this child's birth.

prayer

Father, we ask that You help us to live our faith by loving others, just like the Shunammite woman did. Give us selfless hearts that look at others' needs despite our own unmet longings. Help us to trust You in all the circumstances of our lives. We love You. Amen.

"So, she set out and came to the man of God at Mount Carmel. When he saw her in the distance, the man of God said to his servant Gehazi, 'Look! There's the Shunammite! Run to meet her and ask her, "Are you all right? Is your husband all right? Is your child all right?"' 'Everything is all right,' she said."

2 Kings 4:25–26

Shunammite Woman

Part 2: "faith in the midst of pain"

{Lindsey Jensen}

Flip open the pages to the Old Testament again. Let yourself feel this story by imagining yourself in it. The second part of this woman's story is a nail-biter. In the following paragraphs, I will unfold what I have learned from this story and how I feel God can use this story to teach us lessons we can apply in our own lives.

We learned in the first part of this story that the Shunammite woman did not have a child, and her husband was old. It is inferred that they were unable to have children. But just as Elisha had prophesied, she bore a son.

I can only imagine the celebration they had on the day she saw his sweet face and held him in her arms. A son, the precious baby she had longed to hold.

But this story is not over.

"The child grew, and one day he went out to his father, who was with the reapers. He said to his father, "My head! My head!" His father told a servant, "Carry him to his mother." After the servant had lifted him up and carried him to his mother, the boy sat on her lap until noon, and then he died." (2 Kings 4:18–20)

He died. He died? He died! The first time I heard this story, I could hardly believe this painful twist. I thought this was a miracle child? I thought God had blessed her? Oh, how quickly we lose sight of who our God is and what He can do. I am so guilty. Instead of remembering that our God is the creator of the heavens and earth, the giver of life, and defeater of death, I focus on the circumstances and can hardly see a way out. My heart sinks, and I begin to think about how this woman must have felt. There she sat, holding her young child, no doubt praying with all her might. But her prayers weren't answered. Instead, she held her son as his heart stopped and his breathing subsided.

> She went up and laid him on the bed of the man of God, then shut the door and went out. She called her husband and said, "Please send me one of the servants and a donkey so I can go to the man of God quickly and return."
>
> "Why go to him today?" he asked. "It's not the New Moon or the Sabbath."
>
> "That's all right," she said (2 Kings 4:21–23).

So many things are running through my mind at this point. What stands out to me in this next portion of her story is that she doesn't tell her husband that their son has just died! We aren't told why, but in my opinion, I think she understands the power of faith and the power of the spoken word. She is not willing to proclaim him dead until she goes before the Man of God, the man that God used to give her this miracle child. In this story, we can draw a parallel between the Man of God and the Son of God - although there is only ONE Son of God. At this time in history, Christ had not yet come. Elisha was the closest thing to God that she had known. It did not matter that it wasn't Sunday; nothing would stop her from getting to the Man of God.

> She saddled the donkey and said to her servant, "Lead on; don't slow down for me unless I tell you." So, she set out and came to the man of God at Mount Carmel.
>
> When he saw her in the distance, the man of God said to his servant Gehazi, "Look! There's the Shunammite! Run to meet her and ask her, 'Are you all right? Is your husband all right? Is your child all right?'"
>
> "Everything is all right," she said.
>
> When she reached the man of God at the mountain, she took hold of his feet. Gehazi came over to push her away, but the man of God said, "Leave her alone! She is in bitter distress, but the Lord has hidden it from me and has not told me why."
>
> "Did I ask you for a son, my lord?" she said. "Didn't I tell you, 'Don't raise my

> hopes'?" (2 Kings 4:24–28).

So, the Shunammite woman hurries to see Elisha. This is about a 30-mile trip, and she is on a donkey, which means that this trip took several hours. I can't fathom the immense pain she was feeling.

The Scriptures say Elisha saw her from a distance and told Gehazi (his servant) to run to her and ask if everything was okay with her husband and son. Gehazi does this, and she replies with "Shalom" and pushes past him. Once again, she says, 'everything is just fine.' We don't know exactly why she says this, but maybe it is because she doesn't want to waste a second on someone (or something) that cannot help her—she knows she needs the Man of God, and no one else will do. I have been through times like this. Times when nothing but crying out to God quenches my need for help. When she arrives, we see the same strong and determined woman we met in the beginning of this story. Notice it says, "she took hold of his feet." Once again, her heartbreak is loud and clear. And once again, we see her pushing beyond the rules of religion to encounter God.

This story reminds us that we have a God who wants to hear what is on our hearts. We can approach Him boldly. We can grab hold of His feet! We can wash them with our tears. He knows that in this life, we will have troubles. Have you ever asked God, "Why?! Did I ask for this??" I sure have. Our heavenly Father wants to take away our pain, but the only way He can take it is if you bring it to Him.

> Elisha said to Gehazi, "Tuck your cloak into your belt, take my staff in your hand and run. Don't greet anyone you

meet, and if anyone greets you, do not answer. Lay my staff on the boy's face."

But the child's mother said, "As surely as the Lord lives and as you live, I will not leave you." So, he got up and followed her.

Gehazi went on ahead and laid the staff on the boy's face, but there was no sound or response. So Gehazi went back to meet Elisha and told him, "The boy has not awakened."

When Elisha reached the house, there was the boy lying dead on his couch. He went in, shut the door on the two of them and prayed to the Lord. Then he got on the bed and lay on the boy, mouth to mouth, eyes to eyes, hands to hands. As he stretched himself out on him, the boy's body grew warm. Elisha turned away and walked back and forth in the room and then got on the bed and stretched out on him once more. The boy sneezed seven times and opened his eyes.

Elisha summoned Gehazi and said, "Call the Shunammite." And he did. When she came, he said, "Take your son." She came in, fell at his feet and bowed to the ground. Then she took her son and went out (2 Kings 4:29–36, NIV).

Exhale. Her son is alive! Her prayers were answered.

The Shunammite woman exemplifies the power of faith. She focuses on the unseen and the impossible because she knows that all things are possible with God.

questions

» Why do you think she doesn't tell her husband that their son is dead?

» What is the first thing she does when Elisha tells her that her son is alive? What is the significance of this?

» What are some ways you can profess your faith in something unseen, by words and/or actions?

digging deeper

There is another story in the Old Testament that shows a father who puts faith in God despite the circumstances. Read Genesis 22:1–18. Pay close attention to the pronoun in Genesis 22:5. How does this show incredible faith in the midst of a seemingly horrible situation?

prayer

Father, let us never get tired of coming directly to you. Give us courage to approach you boldly and honestly with pain, fear, anger, or anything we may feel. Help us give these burdens to you and trust in your good character. Teach us to have bold faith like the Shunammite woman displays. Thank you for preserving her story so that we might learn from it. We love you. Amen.

Made in the USA
Columbia, SC
16 June 2025